# NEIL ARMSTRONG
# AND TRAVELLING TO THE MOON

Ben Hubbard

Raintree is an imprint of Capstone Global Library Limited, a company incorporated in England and Wales having its registered office at 7 Pilgrim Street, London, EC4V 6LB – Registered company number: 6695582

www.raintree.co.uk
myorders@raintree.co.uk

Edited by Clare Lewis and Abby Colich
Designed by Steve Mead and Justin Hoffman
Original illustrations © Capstone Global Library Ltd 2015
Illustrated by Justin Hoffman
Picture research by Svetlana Zhurkin
Production by Victoria Fitzgerald
Originated by Capstone Global Library Ltd
Printed and bound in the United Kingdom.

ISBN 978 1 406 29739 3 (hardback)
ISBN 978 1 406 29744 7 (paperback)

**British Library Cataloguing in Publication Data**
A full catalogue record for this book is available from the British Library.

**Acknowledgements**
We would like to thank the following for permission to reproduce photographs:
Alamy: RIA Novosti, 9, The Print Collector, 4; Courtesy of the Ohio History Connection, 7; NASA, cover (top, bottom left), 5, 8, 10, 11, 12, 13, 14, 15, 19, 20, 22—23, 26, 30, 31, 33, 34, 35, 36, 37, 38, 39, 40, 43; Shutterstock: Quaoar, cover (bottom right); University of Cincinnati: Peggy Palange, 41; Wikimedia: Eberhard Marx, 21

We would like to thank Dr Geza Gyuk for his invaluable help in the preparation of this book.

# CONTENTS

All words in bold, **like this**, appear in the glossary on page 45.

# DREAMING OF THE MOON

On 20 July 1969, American **astronaut** Neil Armstrong paused on the bottom rung of his Lunar Module ladder and looked down. "The surface appears to be very, very fine grained as you get close to it; it's almost like a powder," he reported over his helmet radio.

Then, as around 600 million people watched from their television sets on Earth, Armstrong lowered his left foot onto the Moon's surface. He had just become the first human in history to step onto another world. His following words would be forever printed in the history books beside his name: "That's one small step for a man, one giant leap for mankind."

## Lunar stories

Before scientists began working to get astronauts into space, **science fiction** writers made up stories about people being towed to the Moon by geese, or flown aboard hot air balloons. In his 1865 book, *From the Earth to the Moon*, Jules Verne described three men travelling to the Moon on a rocket. This was a remarkable prediction of the *Apollo 11* Moon mission that took place 84 years later.

# TOP PLACE IN SPACE

Sending three astronauts to the Moon aboard *Apollo 11* was one of humanity's greatest accomplishments. However, just 12 years earlier, the United States did not even have the technology to launch a **rocket** into space. At that time, it was losing a race to space against its rival, the **Soviet Union**. Only an ambitious plan like a Moon landing would get the United States on top. All they had to do was design and build the spacecraft and train astronauts to fly in them. Neil Armstrong became the most famous of these astronauts.

Edwin "Buzz" Aldrin is shown stepping onto the Moon to join Neil Armstrong, who is taking the photograph.

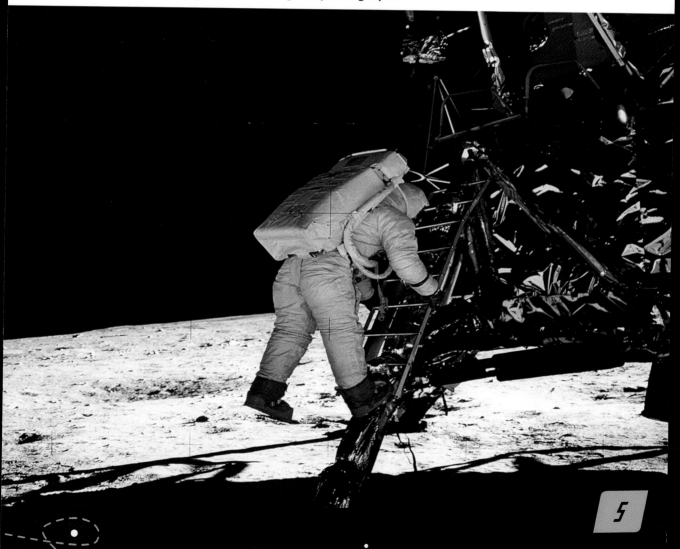

# EARLY FLYER

Neil Alden Armstrong was born in the small town of Wapakoneta, Ohio, on 5 August 1930. He first became fascinated with flying at two years old. This was when his father took him to an air show in Cleveland, Ohio, USA. Armstrong spent his childhood building model planes and working after school to pay for flying lessons.

After graduating from high school, Armstrong studied **aeronautical** engineering at Purdue University. He then flew fighter jets for the US Navy in the Korean War. During one mission, Armstrong had to eject from his jet after being hit by enemy fire from the ground. It was the first of several near misses that Armstrong would experience during his career.

## TEST PILOT

In 1955, Armstrong became a research pilot for the National Advisory Committee for Aeronautics (NACA). He tested helicopters, gliders and over 200 different models of high-speed aircraft. One such aircraft was the rocket-powered *X-15* jet, which could fly at 7,274 kilometres (4,520 miles) per hour. In 1958, NACA turned into the National Aeronautics and Space Administration (NASA) – the agency that would send Armstrong to the Moon.

### SPACE Q AND A

**Q.** What does NASA do?

**A.** NASA is the United States' agency responsible for science and technology related to air and space.

Neil Armstrong as a boy dressed in his marching band uniform.

## Crazy about model planes

Armstrong loved designing and building model planes as a child because it taught him about the science of **aviation**. He was always more interested in reading model aircraft magazines than the science fiction comics, which many American boys enjoyed in the 1950s.

# SENDING MEN TO THE MOON

While Armstrong tested rocket-powered aircraft on Earth, the Soviet Union sent the first rocket into space. The 1957 launch of the Soviet **satellite** *Sputnik 1* stunned the Americans. It meant the Soviets had the technology to fire a long-range missile into the United States. This triggered the competition between the two nations that became known as the Space Race. In 1958, the Americans launched their own satellite, *Explorer 1*, into space. The Soviets responded in 1961 by sending the first man into space: Yuri Gagarin, aboard *Vostok 1*. This news was a terrible blow for the US space programme. Once again, the Soviets had trumped the Americans.

■ **Ham's spacecraft missed its splashdown point in the ocean and nearly sank before the chimpanzee could be rescued.**

### Animal astronaut

The first US astronaut sent into space was not a man, but a chimpanzee. Ham was trained to pull a few simple levers aboard a Mercury spacecraft and was then launched into sub-orbit on 31 January 1961. Ham returned unharmed to Earth 16 minutes later.

■ The Soviet Union's *Vostok 1* blasts off from the Baikonur **Cosmodrome.**

## KENNEDY'S SPACE CHALLENGE

A few weeks after *Vostok 1*, the US launched astronaut Alan Shepard into **sub-orbit** for 15 minutes. This was only a small accomplishment compared to *Vostok 1*, which had **orbited** Earth. However, in May 1961, US president John F. Kennedy announced the most ambitious space plan yet: "This nation should commit itself to achieving the goal, before the decade is out, of landing a man on the Moon and returning him safely to the Earth."

Kennedy's speech shocked the scientists at NASA. They had only just sent an astronaut into space. Now, they had under nine years to get men to the Moon and back again.

# ASTRONAUT ARMSTRONG

In 1962, Armstrong applied to join NASA's space programme. At that time, NASA was busy sending men into Earth's orbit on board its Mercury spacecraft. Now, it was recruiting astronauts for a new type of mission. Armstrong was a perfect match. After being accepted onto the programme, he joined 31 astronaut trainees to undergo advanced tests. During these tests, Armstrong had to keep his foot in a bucket of ice water and had ice water squirted into his ear.

An even harder test was being shut inside an isolation chamber. "There was no sound, no light and no smell. They told you to come out after two hours," Armstrong said. To calculate two hours, Armstrong sang a song over and over again until he thought the time had passed. While this was difficult, the hardest challenge was to follow.

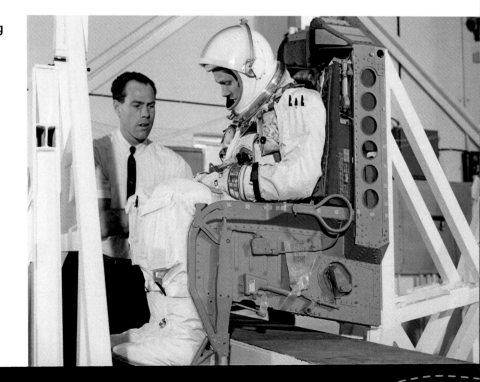

■ Neil Armstrong took part in weight and balance tests as part of his preparation for space.

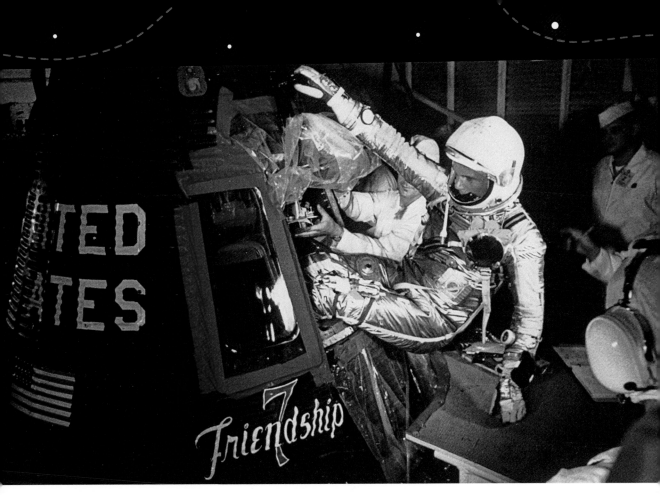

■ Astronaut John Glenn enters *Friendship 7* to begin the first manned US flight around Earth.

## KEEPING COOL IN THE HEAT

For his next test, Armstrong was put into a room where the temperature reached 63 degrees Celsius (145 degrees Fahrenheit). He was then observed to see how he would cope with the extreme heat. Armstrong decided to slow his body down so it would not generate any extra heat. He sat quietly in a corner and did not move. "I don't know how well I did, but I was able to stand it in there," Armstrong said.

### Mercury rising

On 20 February 1962, John Glenn became the first US astronaut to orbit the Earth aboard the Mercury spacecraft, *Friendship 7*. Nearly a year after *Vostok 1*, the US had finally caught up with its Soviet rival.

# THE NEW NINE

Soon after becoming an astronaut trainee, it was announced Armstrong would be one of the "New Nine". They were nine men who would pilot the Gemini missions. As a result of the success of the Mercury missions, Gemini was designed to practise spacewalking and spacecraft **docking**. These were essential to the US plans to send a man to the Moon. To do so, two spacecraft would have to meet up and join together, or "dock", in space. Gemini was NASA's biggest and boldest programme to date. It was bound to be dangerous for the New Nine.

## A walk in space

New Nine astronaut Edward White made the first United States spacewalk aboard *Gemini 4* on 3 June 1965. White was attached to the spacecraft by a cord and used a hand-held "jet gun" to move himself through space. The spacewalk lasted 23 minutes.

■ "I'm coming back in… and it's the saddest moment of my life," said Edward White before ending the first US spacewalk.

## SPACE SPEAK

**Spacewalking:** Also known as an Extra Vehicular Activity, this is when an astronaut leaves his or her spacecraft and moves about in space.

■ An astronaut sat in a cockpit at one end of this centrifuge machine, the NASA Ames 5 Degrees of Motion Simulator.

## BASIC TRAINING

While the Gemini spacecraft were being built, the New Nine were put through basic astronaut training. This included parachute jumps and rides on the dreaded **centrifuge machine**. This machine span an astronaut around at speed so he could experience the high **g-force**, or "G's", felt during lift-off. In total, Armstrong spent five hours on the centrifuge machine and was subject to a high 15 G's.

### Voskhod 2

The Soviet Union beat the United States to carry out the first spacewalk in March 1965. However, the spacewalk almost ended in disaster when **cosmonaut** Aleksey Leonov's over inflated spacesuit nearly prevented him re-entering his *Voskhod 2* spacecraft.

# GEMINI 8

The *Gemini 8* mission was the United States' first attempt to dock a spacecraft with an unmanned rocket in space. As such, NASA needed its most experienced pilot on board, Neil Armstrong. The unmanned rocket – called an Agena Target Vehicle (ATV) – lifted off from Kennedy Space Center on 16 March 1966. *Gemini 8*, carrying Armstrong and astronaut David R Scott, followed 100 minutes later. After six hours, *Gemini 8* caught up to the ATV and successfully docked with it. Now the two spacecraft were flying in space together as one. Then, suddenly, radio contact with *Gemini 8* was lost. When contact was regained 21 minutes later, there were chilling words from the spacecraft: "We have a serious problem here … we're tumbling end over end up here."

## The Cape

The Kennedy Space Center was built in 1950 on a spit of land called Cape Canaveral in Florida, USA. Today, the Center features launch pads, runways, command centres, spacecraft hangers and a seaport.

■ **This photograph shows the Agena Target Vehicle taken from *Gemini 8*, which is around 64 metres (210 feet) away.**

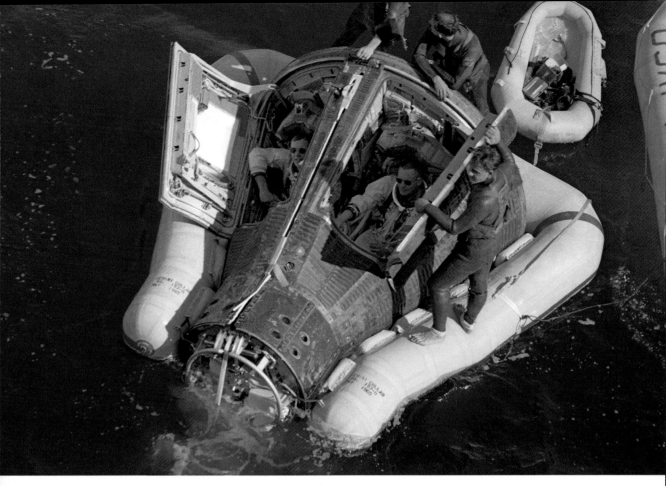

■ *Gemini 8* is retrieved from the ocean after its aborted mission. An inflatable flotation collar keeps the spacecraft steady.

## ARMSTRONG ABORTS

Shortly after docking with the ATV, a jammed thruster on *Gemini 8* had sent both spacecraft into a spin. Armstrong immediately separated *Gemini 8* from the ATV, but the spinning continued. "It was obvious that the problem was not the Agena's. It was ours," Armstrong said.

Worse still, the spinning made Armstrong's vision blurry and he was in danger of passing out. There was only one option: to shut down *Gemini 8*'s thrusters and fire its re-entry rockets to stabilize the spacecraft. The plan worked, but it also meant aborting the mission early. Only 10 hours after it had launched, *Gemini 8* made an emergency splash-down in the Pacific Ocean.

# THE APOLLO PROGRAMME

Despite Armstrong's aborted mission, the Gemini programme was generally a great success for the United States. Now, Gemini was replaced by the programme that would send men to the Moon: Apollo. Time, however, was in short supply. In 1966, Armstrong went on a publicity tour to South America. Meanwhile scientists and designers at NASA worked around the clock to meet President Kennedy's 1969 deadline. Flying men the 382,500 kilometres (237,700 miles) to the Moon would require the most powerful rocket ever built: Saturn V.

## SATURN STAGES

The Saturn V rocket was made up of three smaller rockets, called stages, that fit one on top of the other. Each stage was designed to fire Saturn V a little further into space and then fall away when its fuel was finished.

- Stage 1 would fire for two and a half minutes, boosting Saturn to 68 kilometres (42 miles) above Earth.
- Stage 2 would fire for six minutes, boosting Saturn to 183 kilometres (114 miles) above Earth.
- Stage 3 would fire the Apollo spacecraft to a speed of 11 kilometres (7 miles) per second. This is enough speed for Saturn to leave Earth's orbit and start heading towards the Moon. Sitting above the third stage was the Apollo spacecraft.

## SPACE Q AND A

**Q.** Why the Moon?

**A.** President Kennedy was sure sending men to another world would prove that the United States was superior to the Soviet Union in space. Kennedy's advisers told him the Moon was the most achievable destination.

Apollo spacecraft

Lunar Module

Stage 3

Stage 2

exhaust nozzles

Stage 1

rocket engines

Only the Apollo spacecraft and Lunar Module would reach the Moon after the three *Saturn V* stages burned through their fuel and fell away.

# APOLLO TRAGEDIES

In 1967, the United States suffered its first great space tragedy. On 27 January, astronauts Virgil Grissom, Ed White and Roger Chaffee were killed during testing of *Apollo 1's* Command Module (CM). *Apollo 1* was scheduled to become the first manned Apollo mission into space only a few weeks later. The accident took place during a routine practice run of *Apollo 1's* launch. The three astronauts had boarded the CM and its hatch was bolted on behind them. The countdown was then delayed because of problems with the oxygen supply and radio equipment. Suddenly, a chilling cry came over the radio: "We've got a fire in the cockpit!"

# NO WAY OUT

As a flash fire swept through the CM, the astronauts struggled to open the hatch to get out. From the outside of the CM, the ground crew managed to withstand the intense heat to unbolt the hatch in just a few minutes. But they were too late – the astronauts inside were dead. A report on the accident later found that some safety features may have been overlooked. NASA was in such a hurry to get a man onto the Moon that it had not given enough attention to crew safety. The Apollo programme had faced disaster before it had even got off the ground.

## Cosmonaut killed

The Soviet Union also suffered from a cosmonaut death in 1967. Vladimir Komarov crashed to Earth after the parachute on his *Soyuz 1* spacecraft failed. Many decades later it emerged that around 124 people had also died during a 1960 explosion at the Soviet Baikonur Cosmodrome. The Soviets made sure this "Nedelin Catastrophe" was kept secret at the time.

■ Scorch marks from the intense heat can be seen after the tragedy on *Apollo 1*. Unlike later spacecraft, the Command Module's hatch was not fitted with explosive bolts.

# TRAINING FOR THE MOON

Three days after NASA released its report on the *Apollo 1* tragedy, Armstrong and 17 other astronauts were told they had made the final shortlist for the Moon mission. Armstrong said this put him into an "unspoken competition in which the prize was the ultimate flight test, the first lunar landing".

**Gravity** training for the Moon began immediately. On the Moon there is only one-sixth of the amount of gravity there is on Earth. In space, astronauts do not feel the effects of gravity because they are actually constantly falling. To imitate the low-gravity conditions of the Moon, the astronauts practised walking in their spacesuits in a swimming pool. To practise being **weightless** in space, the astronauts trained aboard a reduced-gravity aircraft. Because the weightless conditions often made the astronauts **nauseous**, the aircraft was nicknamed the "vomit comet".

■ Training in the "Flying Bedstead" gave Armstrong the vital practice needed to land the Lunar Module on the Moon.

## Soviet Lander

The Soviet Union was also working on a Lunar Module in the late 1960s, although the outside world did not see it until 1990. In reality, the module was unlikely to have travelled to the Moon and back. However, news that the Soviets were preparing a manned Moon mission forced the United States to speed up its own plans.

■ The Soviet Lunniy Koarbi (Lunar Craft) was designed to land one man on the Moon, although only unmanned test craft were ever launched.

# LUNAR LANDER

The astronauts also trained aboard the "Flying Bedstead", a practice model of the Lunar Module that would land on the Moon's surface. During his training flight, Armstrong had another near miss when the "Flying Bedstead" span out of control in the air. He was able to eject at the last minute, before the module crashed and exploded into flames.

# APOLLO 8

With fears that the Soviet Union was planning a lunar landing, the United States stepped up its efforts to launch its mission to the Moon. *Apollo 8* would not land on the Moon. Instead, it would circle around it, take photos of its far side (the side of the Moon we can't see from Earth) and fly back to Earth. Although Armstrong was not aboard *Apollo 8*, he was told he would be commander of *Apollo 11*, the first mission to actually land men on the Moon. The countdown to *Apollo 8* began. From "T minus four days and counting", Apollo's 5,000 mission personnel were on high alert, as 60 television cameras beamed pictures of the spacecraft's approaching launch around the world.

## TV missions

Unlike the Soviet space programme, the United States caught every moment of its space missions on camera. On Christmas Eve, 1968, the *Apollo 8* astronauts issued a message of good will that was broadcast live to hundreds of millions of television viewers across the globe.

 **Photographs taken from *Apollo 8* gave people at home a never-seen-before view of the Earth's isolated position in space.**

# EARTHRISE

On 21 December 1968, *Apollo 8* blasted into space. After orbiting Earth once, *Apollo 8*'s rockets fired it to an "escape **velocity**" of 40,000 kilometres (25,000 miles) per hour to send it to the Moon. Less than three days later, *Apollo 8*'s rockets fired again to put it into the Moon's orbit. Those at NASA held their breath as *Apollo 8* travelled around the Moon to its far side – a place never seen by human eyes. Then, to everyone's relief, *Apollo 8* emerged on the other side. The astronauts on board then glimpsed something never seen before by humans: Earth rising above the Moon's horizon.

## SPACE Q AND A

**Q.** What does "T minus", or "T-", mean?

**A.** T minus means the time remaining before a rocket's lift-off.

# Focus on:
# APOLLO 11 SPACECRAFT

By mid-1969, NASA was making its finishing touches to the *Apollo 11* spacecraft that would take Neil Armstrong, Buzz Aldrin and Michael Collins to the Moon. The spacecraft sat on top of the *Saturn V* rocket and was made up of three main parts: the Command Module (CM), the Service Module (SM) and the Lunar Module (LM).

Command Module (CM)

Service Module (SM)

Lunar Module (LM)

■ Although tucked away beneath the Command and Service Modules at launch, the Lunar Module would be unpacked in space before its descent to the Moon.

## Command Module controls

The Command Module's control panels were positioned in front of the astronauts' seats. Primitive by today's standards, the panels consisted of hundreds of switches, lights and simple displays. Altogether, the Command Module had less computing power than a modern mobile phone.

## Lunar Module

The *Apollo 11* Lunar Module was made up of two parts: a **descent** stage at the bottom and an **ascent** stage at the top. The descent stage was fitted with a small engine, four legs and foot pads to land on the Moon, and the equipment which would be used on its surface. The ascent stage was where the astronauts worked and slept. When they had finished their mission, the astronauts would blast off from the Moon in the ascent stage, leaving the descent stage behind. The ascent stage would then re-dock with the CM and SM, which stayed in the Moon's orbit.

docking hatch

astronauts

crew quarters

cargo storage

ascent engine

descent engine

ladder

footpads

# COUNTDOWN BEGINS

With 28 hours to go before the launch of *Apollo 11*, the official countdown began. This was the last chance for the mission controllers to make their final checks. Radio communications, Earth's **tracking stations**, emergency abort systems and weather conditions all had to be checked alongside the Saturn rocket and *Apollo 11* spacecraft.

▇ **The swing arms move away from *Apollo 11* and its *Saturn V* rocket as flames below signal its lift-off.**

# COUNTDOWN

**T–28 hours**
System checks start as the countdown begins.

**T–9 hours**
Fuel is loaded into *Saturn V*.

**T–5 hours, 2 minutes**
The three astronauts, Armstrong, Aldrin and Collins, are examined by a doctor.

**T–4 hours, 32 minutes**
The astronauts eat a final breakfast of coffee, orange juice, scrambled eggs, toast and steak. Hundreds of thousands of people gather at Cape Canaveral to watch the launch.

**T–3 hours, 57 minutes**
The astronauts are helped into their spacesuits. From that point on, they do not breathe fresh air again until returning from the Moon eight days later.

**T–2 hours, 55 minutes**
The astronauts arrive at the launch pad.

**T–2 hours, 40 minutes**
The astronauts board the Command Module of *Apollo 11*. Armstrong settles into the commander's seat and wonders whether the launch will go ahead: "These things were cancelled more often than they were launched. We'd go in, climb out, go back, and get ready for another day," he said.

**T–15 minutes**
Final checks are completed and the Command Module switches to internal power.

**T–9 seconds**
White clouds billow around the rocket's base as the engine ignition begins. In the launch control centre a button saying "LAUNCH COMMIT" is pressed. Fire blasts from the bottom of *Apollo 11* and a deafening boom fills the air.

**T–0 seconds**
A voice from the control centre calls out: "We have lift-off! We have lift-off!"

# LIFT-OFF

As *Apollo 11* blasted into space, the rocket's engines sent out a thunderous roar and shook the astronauts violently in their seats. "In that first 30 seconds it was very hard to hear anything over the radio – even inside the helmet with the headphones," Armstrong said.

After *Apollo 11*'s first and second stages fell away, the conditions slowly became bearable. As the spacecraft entered Earth's orbit, the astronauts got used to working, eating and sleeping in their temporary home. For the three days it took to get to the Moon, the astronauts kept a busy schedule. They prepared the Lunar Module, sent back television broadcasts to Earth and checked their instruments to make sure they were on course.

The *Apollo 11* crew controlled the spacecraft's manoeuvres in space by firing the Service Module's main engines and small thrusters.

**1** *Apollo 11* lifts off, orbits the Earth 1.5 times and discards the first two stages of the *Saturn V* rocket. The third stage fires *Apollo 11* towards the Moon.

**2** The Command Module (CM) and Service Module (SM) detach from *Saturn*'s third stage, turn around and pull out the Lunar Module from inside the third stage. The third stage falls away.

**3** *Apollo 11* orbits the Moon. Armstrong and Aldrin detach in the Lunar Module, called *Eagle*, and land on the Moon. The CM and SM stay in orbit.

**4** The Lunar Module's ascent stage launches from the Moon, re-docks with the Command Module, and is discarded.

**5** The CM and SM blast back towards Earth. The CM separates from the SM and splashes down into the Pacific Ocean.

# THERE AND BACK

The *Apollo 11* spacecraft had to perform a series of manoeuvres to get the astronauts to the Moon and back again. Each manoeuvre had to be timed perfectly, as there was not enough fuel to make mistakes.

# MOON LANDING

With well over half a billion television viewers watching the Moon landing, it was important that nothing went wrong. However, as Armstrong flew the *Eagle* Lunar Module towards the surface, an alarm sounded from its computer. Mission Control in Houston, Texas, USA, told Armstrong to ignore the alarm, but he knew something was not right. *Eagle* had flown past its planned landing spot and was heading for a field of boulders. Worse still, *Eagle*'s fuel gauge had dropped dangerously low and Mission Control warned that *Eagle* had only 60 seconds of fuel left to land. "Thirty seconds," Mission Control called out soon after.

## Mission Control

Mission Control was at the heart of the *Apollo 11* mission. From racks of computers, hundreds of flight controllers monitored every aspect of the mission and kept in constant contact with the astronauts. The radio signal to the Moon was steady, but a three-second delay made long conversations difficult.

■ Buzz Aldrin is pictured with a Solar Wind Composition experiment, shown to his right.

## DIFFICULT DESCENT

Armstrong was NASA's most experienced pilot but he was worried – his heart rate had jumped to a rapid 156 beats per minute. Silence fell over Mission Control as everyone held their breath. At the last possible moment, Armstrong saw a landing spot – a clearing beside a small crater. As he manoeuvred downwards, *Eagle* kicked up grey Moon dust, making it impossible to see the ground. Then, **sensors** on *Eagle*'s footpads detected the surface, and Armstrong let all four pads touch the lunar ground. Seconds later, Mission Control broke into cheers as Armstrong's voice came over the radio: "The *Eagle* has landed."

# FOCUS ON:

# WALKING ON THE MOON

When Armstrong stepped from *Eagle* onto the Moon's surface he united the people watching from Earth in admiration. The Moon, however, was a cold, lonely place with no sign of life. Armstrong's first "small step for a man" was into soft, grey moon dust. "The surface is fine and powdery. I can kick it up loosely with my toe," Armstrong said. Because there is no air or wind on the Moon to blow the dust and soil away, it lay like a blanket over everything.

To breathe outside their *Eagle* Lunar Module, Armstrong and Aldrin had to wear spacesuits. These provided the astronauts with the vital life support systems they needed to survive in the lunar environment.

gold visor

backpack

white outer layer

pressurized second layer

inner layer containing water tubes

## Spacesuits

The *Apollo 11* spacesuit was like a small spacecraft that protected the astronaut inside. An inner layer contained water tubes to keep the astronaut cool and a pressurized second layer formed an airtight seal against space. A white outer layer protected against solar radiation and **micro-meteoroids**. A backpack provided oxygen, controlled the spacesuit's temperature and contained radio communications. A gold visor on the helmet shielded against harsh ultra-violet light from the Sun. On Earth, the bulky spacesuits weighed 81 kilograms (180 pounds), but because of the Moon's low gravity, the astronauts could easily jump around in them.

Armstrong was the first human to make a footprint on the Moon. Because there is no rain or wind on the Moon, it could remain there for millions of years.

## Extreme Moon

Because there is little **atmosphere** on the Moon, it suffers from extreme temperatures. The daytime temperature can reach 121 degrees Celsius (250 degrees Fahrenheit) and at night it can drop to -156 degrees Celsius (-250 degrees Fahrenheit). The Moon has no air to transmit sound, so it is a completely silent world.

# MOON TASKS

After stepping onto the Moon's surface, Armstrong's first task was to collect a rock sample in case they had to take off in a hurry. The rock would provide **geologists** on Earth with important information about the Moon, such as possible signs of life or water. Armstrong and Aldrin then set up equipment to conduct experiments that would be monitored from Earth. One of the experiments measured "Moonquakes" and provided information about the Moon's structure. Another reflected back laser beams from Earth to calculate Earth's exact distance from the Moon.

■ **Armstrong found the best way to take photographs, such as this one of Aldrin, was to mount the camera onto a bracket on the front of his spacesuit.**

■ Among the plaques and medals the Apollo astronauts left on the Moon was this gold olive branch, meant as a symbol of peace.

### Flags and plaques

The astronauts unveiled a plaque commemorating their mission and planted a US flag on the Moon. The flag was designed with a horizontal pole so it looked like it was flapping in the breeze. Armstrong also left a packet of medals in honour of the deceased *Apollo 1* astronauts and the Soviet cosmonauts Vladimir Komarov and Yuri Gagarin.

## CAUGHT ON CAMERA

The astronauts had strict instructions to catch their whole Moon expedition on camera. They used black and white television cameras to transmit footage back to Earth. They had photographic cameras to take pictures of themselves and their surroundings. Aldrin took only one photograph of Armstrong, showing his back. The only time his image was captured clearly was when it was reflected in the visor of Buzz Aldrin's helmet. "I don't think Buzz had any reason to take my picture, and it never occurred to me that he should. I have always said Buzz was the far more photogenic of the crew," Armstrong said.

# EARTH BOUND

After only two hours and 31 minutes on the Moon's surface, Armstrong and Aldrin climbed back aboard *Eagle*. Their mission now over, the astronauts had to prepare for the voyage home. Once back inside *Eagle*, they changed out of their spacesuits and ate a meal. However, the grey Moon dust had got into everything and made the air smell like wet ash. The astronauts had to once again put on their spacesuits to throw away anything they didn't need. Dust-covered space boots, empty food packages and small bags of human waste were thrown out from *Eagle*, creating the first lunar litter.

After the astronauts had a short sleep, *Eagle*'s ascent stage blasted off from the Moon to dock with Collins in the Command and Service Module. Collins had been alone for some of the time with no radio contact while Armstrong and Aldrin were on the Moon. Now, as Collins helped his dusty colleagues back into the Module, Armstrong passed him the precious cargo of Moon rock and soil.

■ Buzz Aldrin shows the TV audience on Earth how to make a sandwich in space. At this time, the Apollo spacecraft was around 220,000 kilometres (137,000 miles) from Earth.

## Space food

Astronaut food was pre-cooked, freeze-dried and packaged in meal-sized airtight bags or tubes. Some of the meals were ready to eat and others required hot water. In weightless space, it was important that no crumbs or liquid floated from a food bag and interfered with the equipment. As such, the meals included chocolate pudding and beef and vegetable paste.

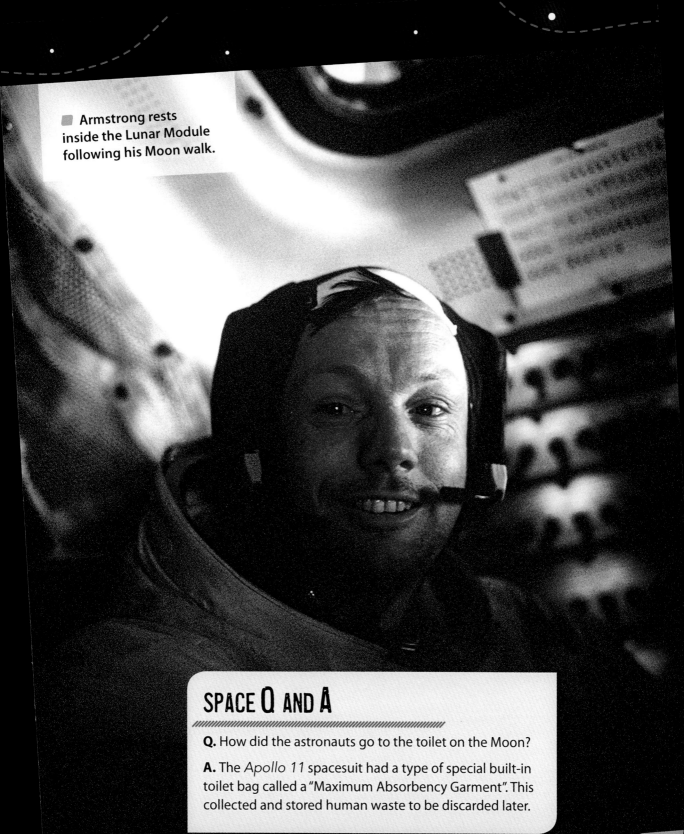

Armstrong rests inside the Lunar Module following his Moon walk.

## SPACE Q AND A

**Q.** How did the astronauts go to the toilet on the Moon?

**A.** The *Apollo 11* spacesuit had a type of special built-in toilet bag called a "Maximum Absorbency Garment". This collected and stored human waste to be discarded later.

# SPLASH-DOWN

After nearly three days of travelling through space, *Apollo 11* neared Earth. Landing, however, was as dangerous as lift-off. After separating from the Service Module, the Command Module hit Earth's atmosphere at a whopping 40,000 kilometres (25,000 miles) per hour. As the module tore through the clouds, its orange and white parachutes flapped open. The parachutes stabilized the module, but as it hit the Pacific Ocean hard each astronaut let out a loud grunt. After bobbing around in the rough water, Navy frogmen (divers) helped the astronauts from Apollo's hatch into rescue rafts. Their mission was complete.

■ US president Richard Nixon visits the *Apollo 11* astronauts in their quarantine trailer.

■ The people of New York line the streets to welcome home the *Apollo 11* astronauts in one of the largest parades in the city's history.

## MOON GERMS

Nobody was sure if the astronauts had been exposed to any dangerous germs on the Moon that could harm people on Earth. So, the astronauts were put into a quarantine trailer for 16 days. Inside, a phone enabled the astronauts to speak to their families. One of Armstrong's first calls was to his mother: "Hello, Mom, this is Neil … all three of us are just fine … none of us got sick and all of the machinery worked. It was fantastically beautiful. The surface is covered with a black dust, and it got all over our nice, clean white suits and wouldn't brush off."

### World celebration

After being given a clean bill of health, the astronauts left the quarantine trailer to a new life as world celebrities. They embarked on a 45-day "Giant Leap" tour around the world, which included state dinners, TV interviews and ticker-tape parades. However, like cosmonaut Yuri Gagarin who came before them, the Apollo astronauts often found their new-found fame difficult to handle.

# LIFE AFTER APOLLO

The US Moon missions did not end with *Apollo 11*. Between 1969 and 1972, five more Apollo spacecraft landed on the Moon. Ten more astronauts walked on the lunar surface. Neil Armstrong, however, was not among them. Instead, Armstrong was expected to be the US poster boy for space. This meant many official dinners and talking engagements in the United States and abroad. Armstrong even travelled to Russia to meet the first woman into space, Valentina Tereshkova, and Yuri Gagarin's widow. Armstrong told Valentina Gagarina he had left a medal honouring her husband on the Moon.

■ **Armstrong was awarded the first Congressional Space Medal of Honor.**

## Apollo 13

In 1970, the US space programme was shaken when *Apollo 13* had to abort its mission to the Moon. The spacecraft was damaged by an explosion in its oxygen tank 320,000 kilometres (200,000 miles) from Earth. The crew only just made it home alive by using the air on board the spacecraft's Lunar Module.

■ Armstrong explains the science of spaceflight to engineering students in 1974.

# AFTER NASA

Armstrong was something of a reluctant celebrity and retired from NASA in 1971. His fascination with aviation had started with the model aircraft magazines he'd read as a boy. After NASA, Armstrong decided to use his knowledge to teach Aerospace Engineering at the University of Cincinnati in Ohio, USA. He later worked as a spokesman for several US businesses and as a spaceflight accident investigator. Armstrong's fame never let him stray far from public view, but he didn't like to profit from his celebrity status. He hired a full-time secretary to help answer his many letters, but stopped sending autographs after some were put up for sale on eBay. Armstrong also made his barber pay £1,850 ($3,000) to charity after he sold a lock of his hair. In 2012, Neil Armstrong died after a heart operation. He was 82 years old.

# MISSION ACCOMPLISHED?

In 1969, *Apollo 11* completed President Kennedy's dream of "landing a man on the Moon before the decade is out". The mission had been designed to beat the Soviet Union in space. However, after this had been achieved it was unclear what the next challenge should be. Throughout the Apollo missions, the United States had been a nation in a state of turmoil. It was fighting an unpopular war in Vietnam and there was great social unrest at home. Many considered the Moon missions wasteful, when people were struggling for their basic human rights on Earth. In 1972, the Apollo programme was cancelled and the *Apollo 17* astronauts were the last men to walk on the Moon.

## FINDING PEACE IN SPACE

The Apollo programme, often called the "greatest technological achievement in human history", cost over £12.3 billion. However, it was anything but a waste of money. It provided enormous breakthroughs in technology, such as the development of the microchip used in all modern computing. It showed that humans are capable of travelling long distances in space and surviving on other worlds. It also paved the way for cooperation between old enemies. In 1970, the docking of the *Apollo–Soyuz* spacecrafts put an end to the Space Race, as Russians and Americans extended the hand of peace in space.

Neil Armstrong described the Earth from the Moon as "big, and bright, and beautiful". Hopefully, one legacy of future space programmes is for all nations to recognize the need for peace on Earth as we continue to explore space.

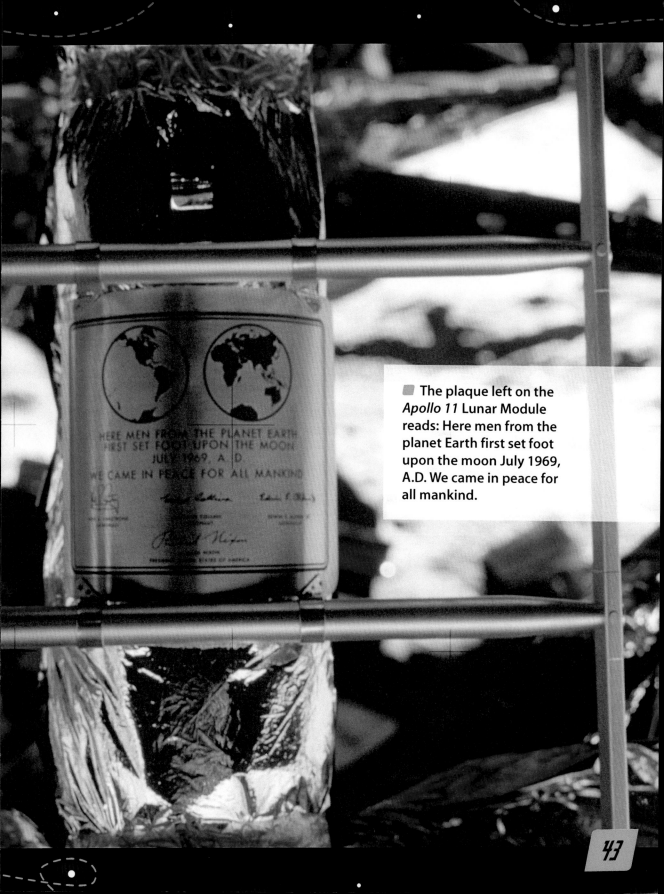

The plaque left on the *Apollo 11* Lunar Module reads: Here men from the planet Earth first set foot upon the moon July 1969, A.D. We came in peace for all mankind.

# TIMELINE

**5 August 1930**     Neil Armstrong is born in Wapakoneta, Ohio, USA

**1952**     Armstrong becomes a research pilot for the National Advisory Committee for Aeronautics (NACA)

**1955**     Armstrong becomes a test pilot for NACA

**1957**     The Soviet Union launches satellite *Sputnik 1* into orbit around Earth

**1958**     The US launches its first satellite, *Explorer 1*

**12 April 1961**     Cosmonaut Yuri Gagarin becomes the first man into space aboard *Vostok 1*

**5 May 1961**     US astronaut Alan Shepard is launched into sub-orbit for 15 minutes aboard *Freedom 7*

**25 May 1961**     President John F. Kennedy announces that the United States will land a man on the Moon by the end of the decade

**1962**     Armstrong becomes one of NASA's "New Nine" astronauts selected for the Gemini missions

**20 February 1962**     John Glenn becomes the first American to orbit Earth aboard the Mercury spacecraft, *Friendship 7*

**16 March 1966**     Armstrong has to abort the *Gemini 8* mission when the spacecraft is put into a spin after docking with the Agena rocket

**27 January 1967**     Astronauts Virgil Grissom, Ed White and Roger Chaffee are killed during testing of *Apollo 1*

**21 December 1968**     *Apollo 8* makes the first manned trip into the Moon's orbit and back

**20 July 1969**     Neil Armstrong becomes the first man to step foot on the Moon, as commander of the *Apollo 11* mission

**1970**     The United States and the Soviet Union join forces in space. This enables the docking of the *Apollo–Soyuz* spacecrafts in 1975.

**1971**     Armstrong retires from NASA

**1972**     The last NASA astronauts land on the Moon as the Apollo programme is cancelled

**2012**     Neil Armstrong dies at 82 years old

# GLOSSARY

**aeronautical** science that deals with aeroplanes and flying

**ascent** act of rising upwards

**astronaut** person trained to travel into space aboard a spacecraft

**atmosphere** protective layer of air and other gases that surrounds Earth, allowing living things to survive

**aviation** flying or operating aircraft

**centrifuge machine** spinning machine that inflicts a high g-force on a cosmonaut or astronaut

**Cosmodrome** Soviet launching site for rockets and other spacecraft

**cosmonaut** astronaut belonging to the Russian, or former Soviet Union, space programme

**descent** falling or moving downwards

**docking** two spacecraft joining in space

**geologist** scientist who studies rocks and soil

**g-force** short for gravity-force, a force of gravity, high loads of which are felt during rapid acceleration

**gravity** pulling force that attracts objects to one another

**micro-meteoroid** very small object moving in space, often made of rock

**nauseous** feeling like you are about to vomit

**orbit** curved path an object follows around a planet, or other celestial body, as a result of its gravity

**rocket** cylindrical object that is driven upwards by burning fuel and expelling the gases to provide propulsion

**satellite** object that orbits a star, planet or asteroid. Satellites can be natural, such as the Moon, or man-made, such as *Sputnik 1*.

**science fiction** fiction based in the future or on different worlds

**sensor** device that detects and records heat, sound or movement. Sensor pads can be used in medicine to measure a person's pulse.

**Soviet Union** (full name, the Union of Soviet Socialist Republics, or USSR), union of Russia and 14 surrounding states, dissolved in 1991

**sub-orbit** a path that does not complete a full orbit of Earth or other planet

**tracking station** place that monitors the movement of spacecraft, ships or aircraft using radar

**velocity** an object's speed

**weightless** something that is weightless is not held down by gravity. In space, the force of gravity is not felt.

# FIND OUT MORE

## BOOKS

*Spacecraft* (Technology Timelines), Tom Jackson (Franklin Watts, 2015)
*Space Pioneers* (The Story of Space), Steve Parker (Franklin Watts, 2015)
*The Moon* (Astronaut Travel Guides), Chris Oxlade (Raintree, 2012)
*What does space exploration do for us?* (Earth, Space, and Beyond),
    Neil Morris (Raintree, 2011)

## DVDs

*For All Mankind* (2010)
This is a documentary about the Apollo Programme compiled from the astronauts' own footage shot during the missions.

*In the Shadow of the Moon* (2008)
The Apollo astronauts discuss the Moon missions in this documentary by Ron Howard.

*Moonwalk One* (2009)
This documentary is about the first Moon landing and *Apollo 11*, and features interviews with its astronauts.

*Stephen Hawking's Universe* (2010)
The world-famous cosmologist explores the mysteries of the Universe, including the Big Bang, the origins of the Universe and the search for extraterrestrial life.

## PLACES TO VISIT

Kennedy Space Center, Florida, USA

**www.kennedyspacecenter.com/**
The Kennedy Space Center features exhibits about space technology and observation gantries that look down on the rocket launch sites and the launch control centre.

National Space Centre, Leicester
**www.spacecentre.co.uk**
This is a visitor complex dedicated to information about space, astronomy and space explorations. The Space Centre houses six space galleries, a film theatre, and a planetarium.

Smithsonian National Air and Space Museum, New York, USA

**airandspace.si.edu/**

The Smithsonian has a special exhibition dedicated to the Apollo Programme, which includes a *Saturn V* engine and a Lunar Roving Vehicle.

The Euro Space Centre, Transinne, Belgium

**www.eurospacecenter.be/esc**

The Euro Space Centre features hands-on space experiments and several spacecraft simulators, as part of its teaching about the European space programme and its contribution to the International Space Station.

# WEBSITES

**www.apolloarchive.com/apollo_gallery.html**

This is a huge database of images from the Apollo programme, from Ham the Chimp through to Apollo 17.

**www.esa.int/esaKIDSen/**

This is the European Space Programme page created just for young people. It gives background information on the Universe as well as space exploration.

**www.nasa.gov/audience/forstudents**

This is the National Aeronautics and Space Administration's (NASA) homepage dedicated to providing information for younger learners on current and historical missions, and space development work.

**www.ustream.tv/channel/live-iss-stream**

Find a live stream of the International Space Station, showing internal views of the station and external views of the Earth.

# HOW CAN I FIND OUT MORE?

Look in more detail at the lives of the other figures involved in the US side of the Space Race. Wernher von Braun was a controversial figure who had built the V-2 rocket for Germany during World War II. He then designed the *Saturn V* for the United States following World War II.

Compare the roles of today's astronauts with those during the Mercury, Gemini and Apollo programmes. The United States' early astronauts often suffered from their celebrity status following their space missions, such as *Apollo 11*'s Buzz Aldrin. Today's astronauts, such as Chris Hadfield, are more prepared for fame.

# INDEX